Calypso

Calypso is a Fren⟨ the Caribbean Isl⟨ the 1950s. It was ⟨ form played by large ensembles until the appearance of the steel drums. Nowadays, the Calypso rhythm can be heard in both steel drum ensembles and various other small-band groups.

Drumset

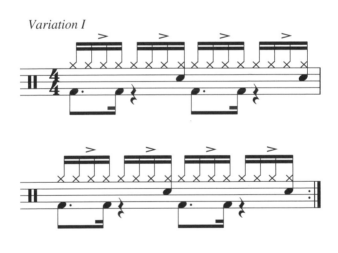

Variation I

Variation II

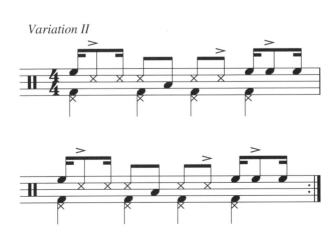

Cáscara

Cáscara ("shell" or "peel") is the name given to the specific pattern that is played on the side of the timbales or conga (shell). Cáscara is usually played during the verses in the *salsa* (modern son).

With 3-2 rumba clave

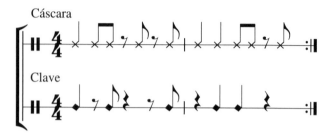

Variation with taps on timbal

With 2-3 rumba clave

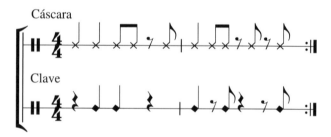

Variation with taps on timbal

Caterete

Caterete is a samba-based folk rhythm from Brazil.

Congas

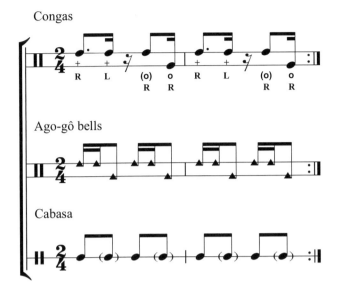

Ago-gô bells

Cabasa

Drumset

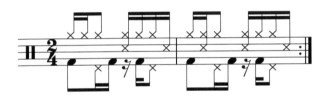

Cha-cha-chá

Cha-cha-chá was a popular dance in Cuba during the 1950s. Charanga orchestras comprised of piano, flute, violins, bass and timbales usually played this style.

Güiro

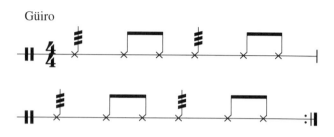

Congas

Timbales

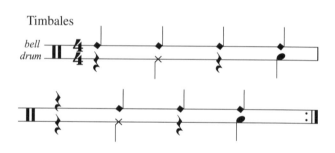

Drumset

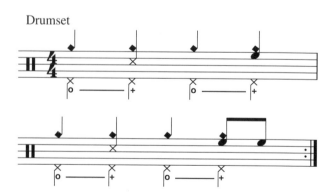

Changüí

Changüí is one of the oldest Cuban genres. It originated in the early nineteenth century in the eastern region of the Guantánamo province. It combines elements of the Spanish *canción* with African rhythms and percussion instruments. The *tres* is essential to the changüí sound, which is thought to be the predecessor of modern son (or *son montuno*).

In 2/4
Guayo (Güiro)

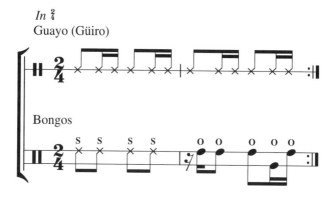

Bongos

In 4/4
Guayo (Güiro)

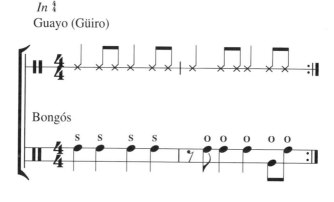

Bongós

Clave

The term *clave* means "key," and for this reason is the most important rhythm in Afro-Cuban music. Whether **obvious** (sounding) or **implicit** (not sounding), the clave is always (as with most of these rhythms) present in the different Afro-Cuban rhythms and percussion patterns. The typical instrument used to play it is also called the *claves*, which is made of two pieces of wood that are struck to one another. The clave can be played on different instruments, such as on the side of timbales, congas, drumset, etc.

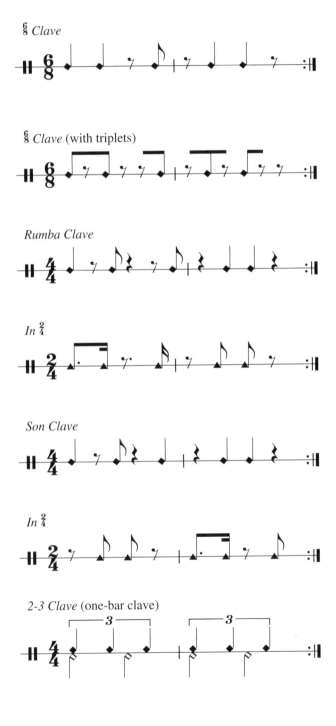

$\frac{6}{8}$ *Clave*

$\frac{6}{8}$ *Clave* (with triplets)

Rumba Clave

In $\frac{2}{4}$

Son Clave

In $\frac{2}{4}$

2-3 Clave (one-bar clave)

Conga

Conga is a traditional Cuban rhythm that is played during the *comparsa* (or carnival) festival, usually played in large ensembles of percussionists, brass players, dancers and singers.

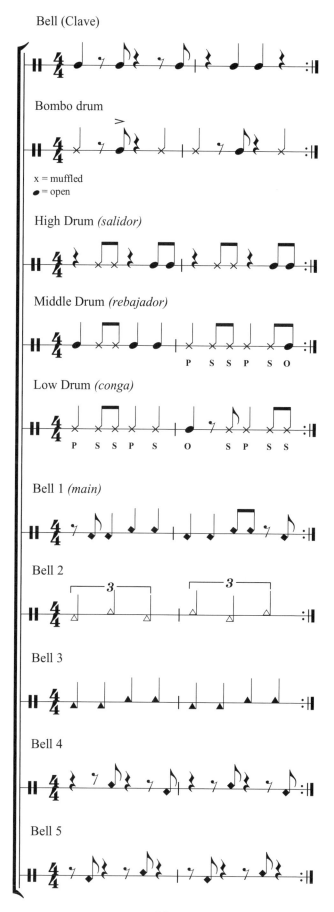

Cumbia

Cumbia is one of the most popular Latin-American rhythms. The original folk cumbia originated on the North Atlantic coast of Colombia and was originally played with flutes, drums and accordion.

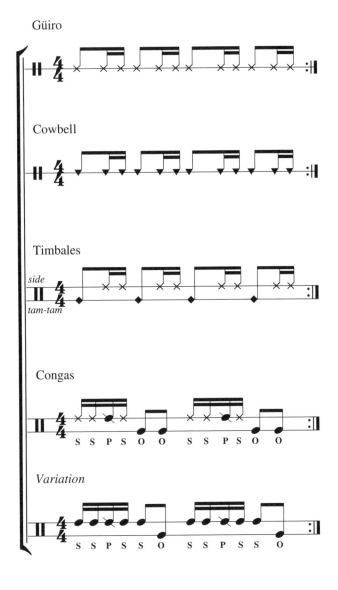

Güiro

Cowbell

Timbales

side

tam-tam

Congas

S S P S O O   S S P S O O

Variation

S S P S S O   S S P S S O

Drumset

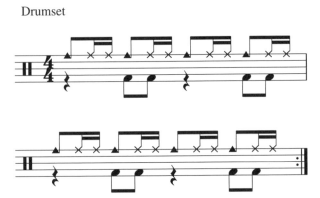

Danzón

Danzón is an Afro-Cuban rhythm with French influences (*contredanse*). This rhythm developed from a popular slow-dance form. In its more traditional form, danzón rhythm usually has a section played by violin and flute. The most important percussion instruments in the danzón are the claves and the timbal (timbale; **F** = finger tap).

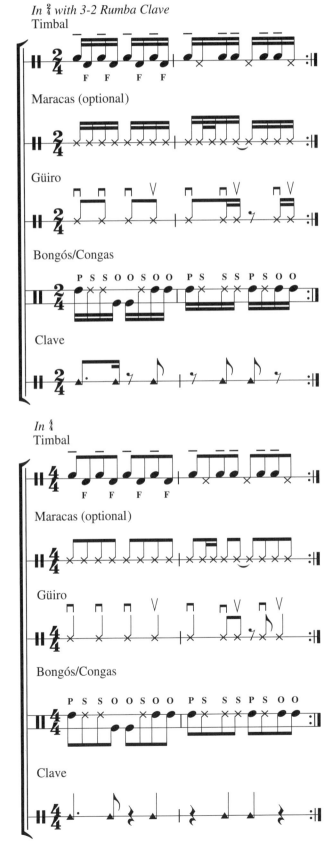

In ²/₄ with 3-2 Rumba Clave

Forró

Forró is a northeastern Brazilian rhythm. The traditional instrumentation for this style consists of accordion, zabumba and triangle. Forró is closely associated with samba, but is not quite the same. The emphasis of this rhythm falls on the first beat of every measure.

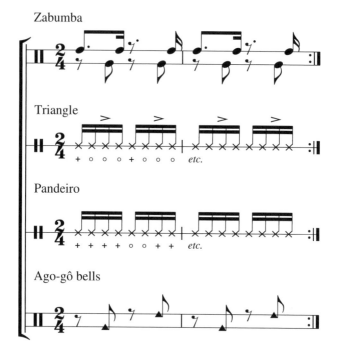

Frevo

Frevo is a kind of march from Recife, Pernambuco, in northeast Brazil. This rhythm is usually played with a fast and light feel.

Guaguancó

This is the most popular form of the *rumba*, which is a folkloric Cuban rhythm. The drums used in the rhythm are: *quinto*, *salidor*, and tres (or *tres golpes*).

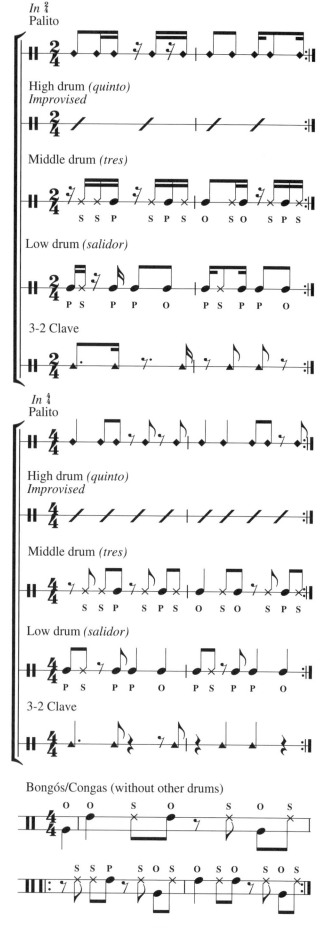

Guaracha

Guaracha is one of the earliest forms of street music, and has satirical lyrics. A traditional Cuban peasant folk rhythm, the rhythmic structure of the guaracha resembles the traditional son style. The term guaracha is now widely used to mean a medium-tempo son.

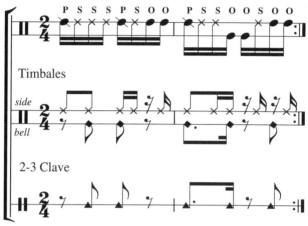

Kiribá

Kiribá is one of the oldest and most traditional Cuban styles. It is a lyric and improvisational form typically played with tres, bongós, maracas, güiro and marímbula. Kiribá is widely played in Guantánamo province.

In $\frac{2}{4}$

Guayo (Güiro)

Bongós

Bell

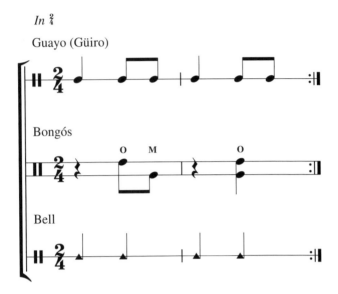

In $\frac{4}{4}$ (double time)

Guayo (Güiro)

Bongós

Bell

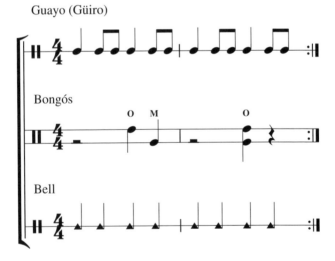

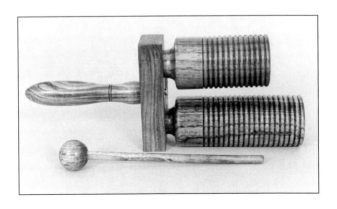

Mambo

Mambo is an Afro-Cuban rhythm that was very popular in the 1940s and '50s. It is the result of one of the early fusions in modern Cuban instrumentation, since it is usually played with a large brass section (sometimes even with a big band). Pérez Prado was one of the main ambassadors of mambo music. He took his music first to Mexico and then to New York City, where it achieved worldwide recognition.

Maracatú

Maracatú was a procession rhythm used during the coronation ceremony for African kings. This rhythm is one of the most energetic, yet steady styles of Brazilian music. The use of a zabumba, a very large *bombo*—or bass drum—enhances the overall festive feeling.

Zabumba

Ago-gô bells

Triangle

Caxixi

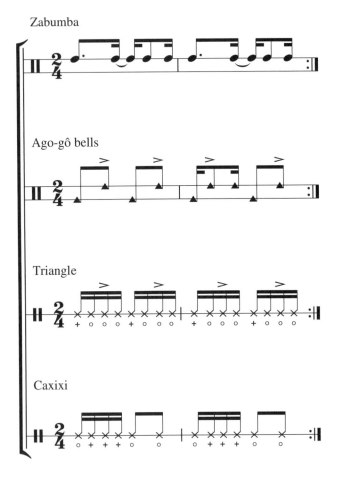

Drumset

Calypso

Calypso is a French rhythm that originated in the Caribbean Islands (most likely Trinidad) in the 1950s. It was originally a folk-type song form played by large ensembles until the appearance of the steel drums. Nowadays, the Calypso rhythm can be heard in both steel drum ensembles and various other small-band groups.

Drumset

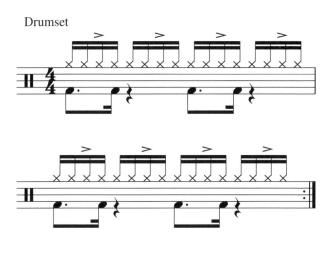

Variation I

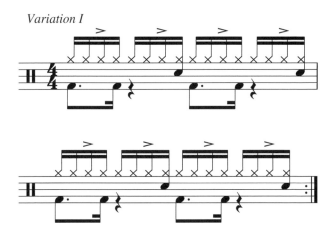

Variation II

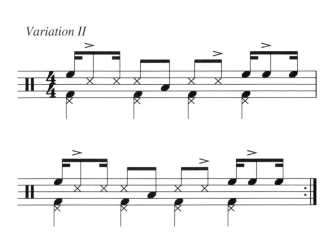

Cáscara

Cáscara ("shell" or "peel") is the name given to the specific pattern that is played on the side of the timbales or conga (shell). Cáscara is usually played during the verses in the *salsa* (modern son).

With 3-2 rumba clave

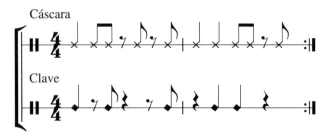

Variation with taps on timbal

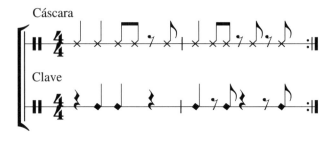

With 2-3 rumba clave

Variation with taps on timbal

Caterete

Caterete is a samba-based folk rhythm from Brazil.

Congas

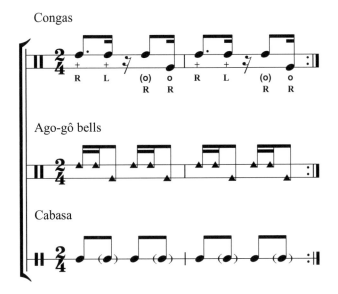

Drumset

Cha-cha-chá

Cha-cha-chá was a popular dance in Cuba during the 1950s. Charanga orchestras comprised of piano, flute, violins, bass and timbales usually played this style.

Güiro

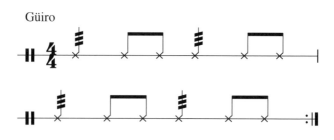

Congas

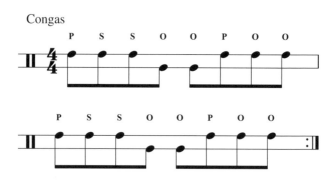

Timbales

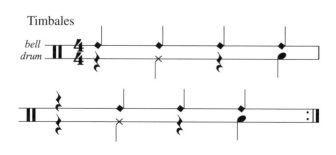

Drumset

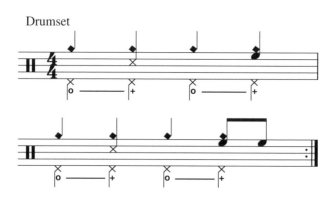

Changüí

Changüí is one of the oldest Cuban genres. It originated in the early nineteenth century in the eastern region of the Guantánamo province. It combines elements of the Spanish *canción* with African rhythms and percussion instruments. The *tres* is essential to the changüí sound, which is thought to be the predecessor of modern son (or *son montuno*).

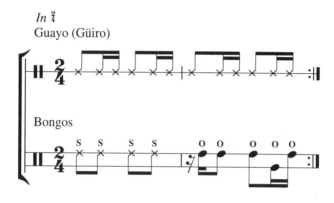

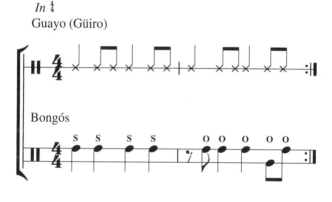

Clave

The term *clave* means "key," and for this reason is the most important rhythm in Afro-Cuban music. Whether **obvious** (sounding) or **implicit** (not sounding), the clave is always (as with most of these rhythms) present in the different Afro-Cuban rhythms and percussion patterns. The typical instrument used to play it is also called the *claves*, which is made of two pieces of wood that are struck to one another. The clave can be played on different instruments, such as on the side of timbales, congas, drumset, etc.

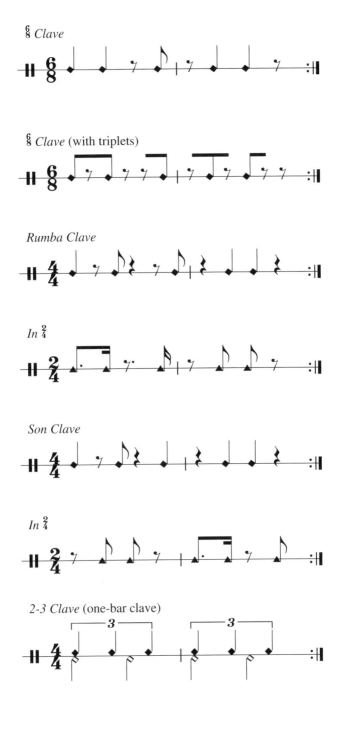

§ *Clave*

§ *Clave* (with triplets)

Rumba Clave

In ⅔

Son Clave

In ⅔

2-3 Clave (one-bar clave)

Conga

Conga is a traditional Cuban rhythm that is played during the *comparsa* (or carnival) festival, usually played in large ensembles of percussionists, brass players, dancers and singers.

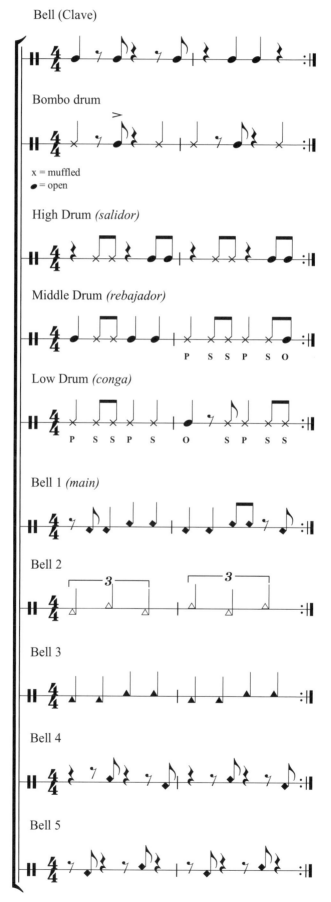

Cumbia

Cumbia is one of the most popular Latin-American rhythms. The original folk cumbia originated on the North Atlantic coast of Colombia and was originally played with flutes, drums and accordion.

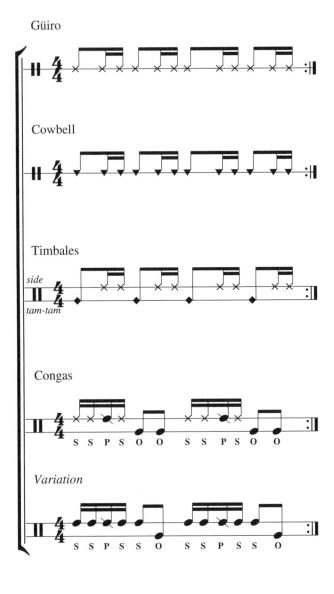

Güiro

Cowbell

Timbales

Congas

Variation

Drumset

Danzón

Danzón is an Afro-Cuban rhythm with French influences (*contredanse*). This rhythm developed from a popular slow-dance form. In its more traditional form, danzón rhythm usually has a section played by violin and flute. The most important percussion instruments in the danzón are the claves and the timbal (timbale; **F** = finger tap).

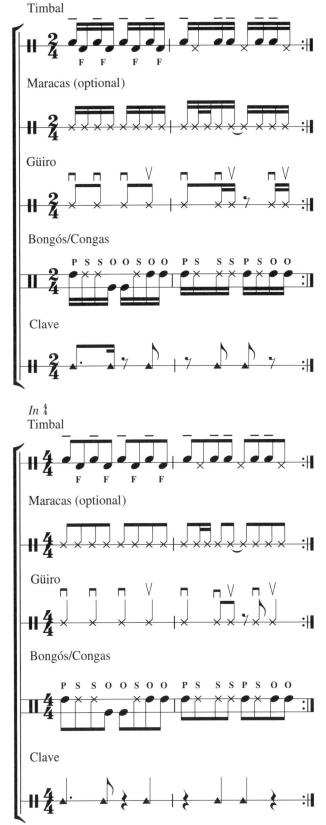

25

Forró

Forró is a northeastern Brazilian rhythm. The traditional instrumentation for this style consists of accordion, zabumba and triangle. Forró is closely associated with samba, but is not quite the same. The emphasis of this rhythm falls on the first beat of every measure.

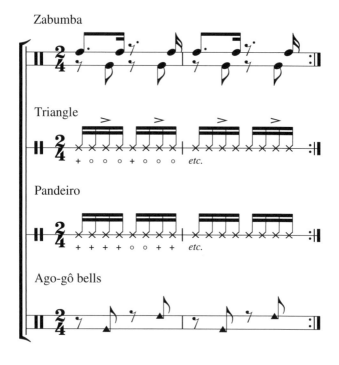

Frevo

Frevo is a kind of march from Recife, Pernambuco, in northeast Brazil. This rhythm is usually played with a fast and light feel.

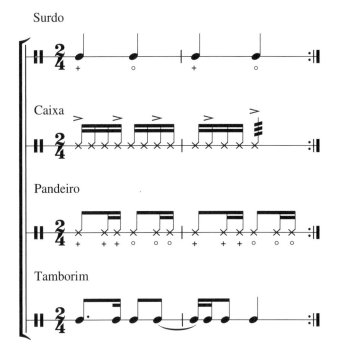

Guaguancó

This is the most popular form of the *rumba*, which is a folkloric Cuban rhythm. The drums used in the rhythm are: *quinto*, *salidor*, and tres (or *tres golpes*).

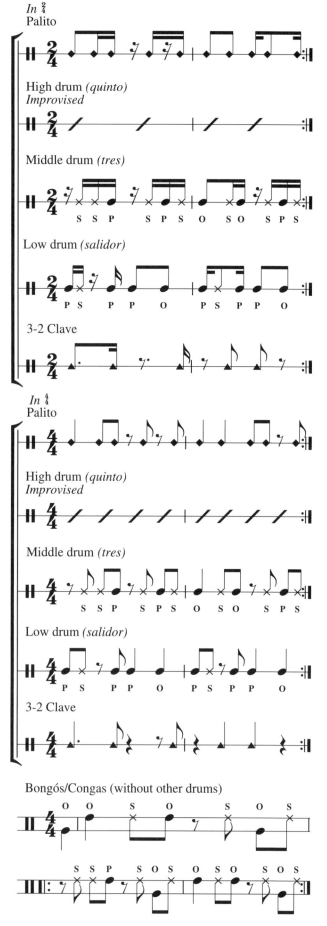

Bongós/Congas (without other drums)

Guaracha

Guaracha is one of the earliest forms of street music, and has satirical lyrics. A traditional Cuban peasant folk rhythm, the rhythmic structure of the guaracha resembles the traditional son style. The term guaracha is now widely used to mean a medium-tempo son.

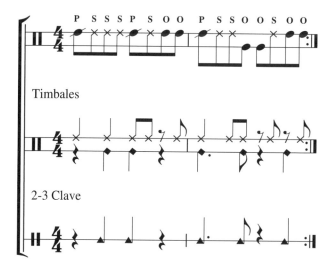

Kiribá

Kiribá is one of the oldest and most traditional Cuban styles. It is a lyric and improvisational form typically played with tres, bongós, maracas, güiro and marímbula. Kiribá is widely played in Guantánamo province.

In ²⁄₄

Guayo (Güiro)

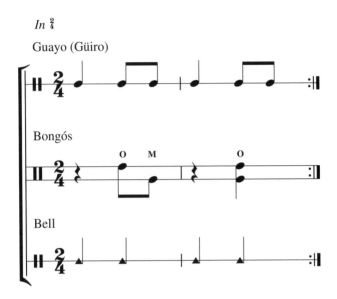

In ⁴⁄₄ (double time)

Guayo (Güiro)

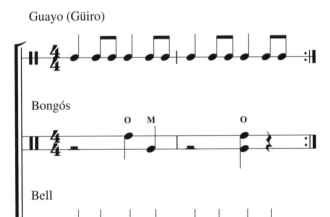

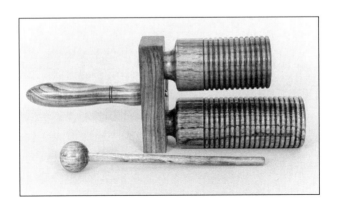

Mambo

Mambo is an Afro-Cuban rhythm that was very popular in the 1940s and '50s. It is the result of one of the early fusions in modern Cuban instrumentation, since it is usually played with a large brass section (sometimes even with a big band). Pérez Prado was one of the main ambassadors of mambo music. He took his music first to Mexico and then to New York City, where it achieved worldwide recognition.

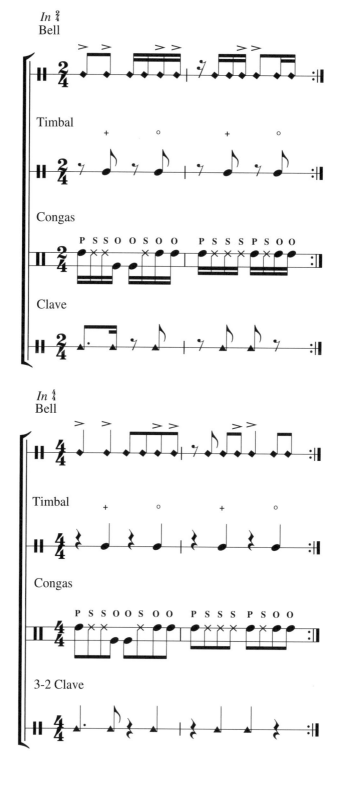

Maracatú

Maracatú was a procession rhythm used during the coronation ceremony for African kings. This rhythm is one of the most energetic, yet steady styles of Brazilian music. The use of a zabumba, a very large *bombo*—or bass drum—enhances the overall festive feeling.

Zabumba

Ago-gô bells

Triangle

Caxixi

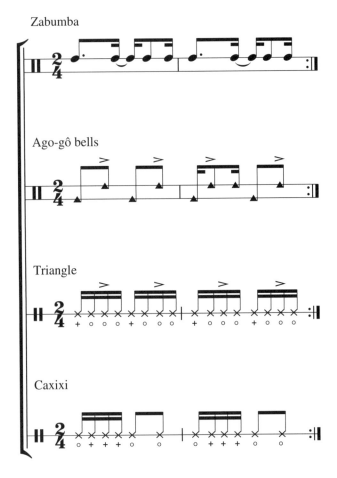

Drumset

Merengue

Merengue is a folk dance and rhythm from the Dominican Republic with strong African and French roots. Merengue has three main parts: *merengue*, *jaleo*, and *apanpichao*. Its typical instrumentation includes: tambora, güiro, and accordion.

In 2/4
Güiro

Tambora

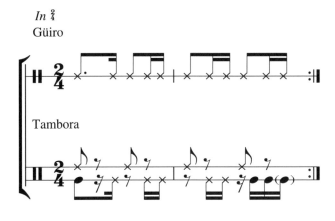

In 4/4
Güiro

Tambora

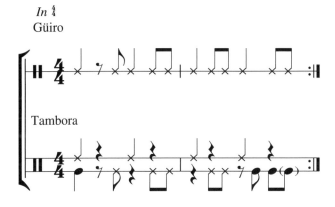

Drumset

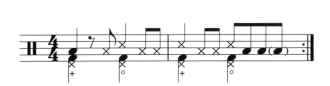

Mozambique

Mozambique is a contemporary Afro-Cuban style created by Pedro Izquierdo (Pelo el Afrokan) around 1960. This rhythm combines traditional African and Afro-Cuban rhythms.

In ²⁄₄

Timbal

Bongós/Congas

2-3 Rumba Clave

In ⁴⁄₄

Timbal

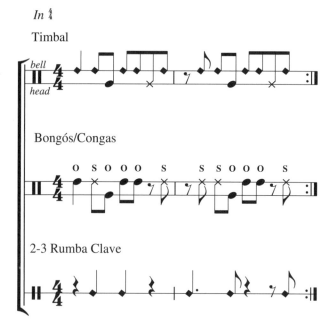

Bongós/Congas

2-3 Rumba Clave

Drumset

Nanigo

Nanigo is an Afro-Cuban secular dance loosely based on the forms and motifs of the abakwa rhythm. It is played with a large percussion ensemble, and is often played as a break section in son music.

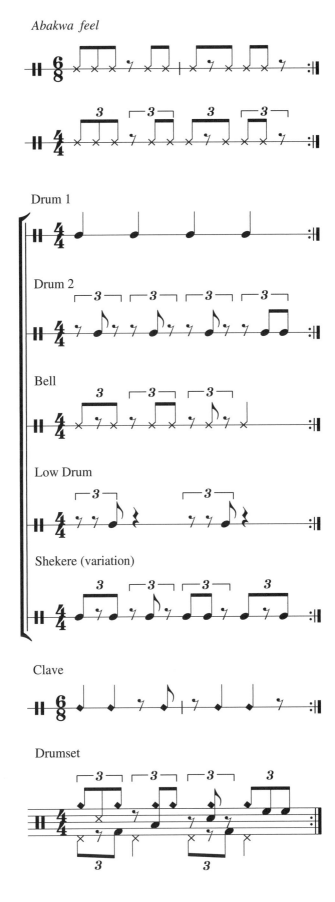

Nengón

Nengón originated in Baracoa, a municipality of the Guantánamo province, and is known to be the precursor to both son montuno and changüí. Nengón was traditionally played with a *tingotalango* or *tumbandera* (a bass instrument made with a tree and rope). Nengón is a simple, melodic folk form based on two chords. The singer improvises the verses and alternates with the choruses.

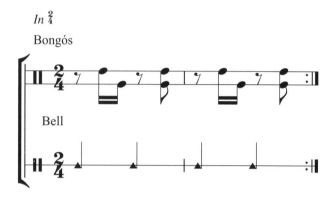

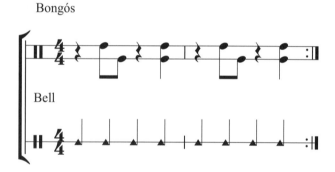

Norteño

Norteño is a combination of Czech and German rhythms that influenced the folk music in the northern region of Mexico. This style is very diverse and has a lot of variations, among the most popular: *ranchera, conjunto, banda, quebradita, corrido,* and *tejano*.

Standard

Variation

Variation (with brushes)

Quebradita

Palito

Palito is the Spanish name for "little stick."
This rhythm is the predecessor of the cáscara
pattern and was originally played on an
instrument called a *gua-gua,* which was a
clave-style instrument made of bamboo. This
rhythm is emblematic of the rumba style.

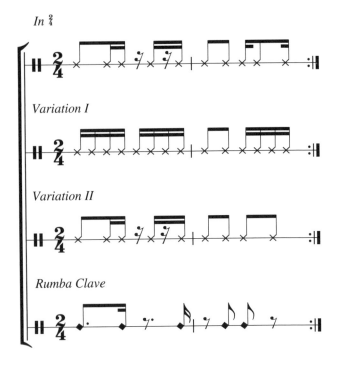

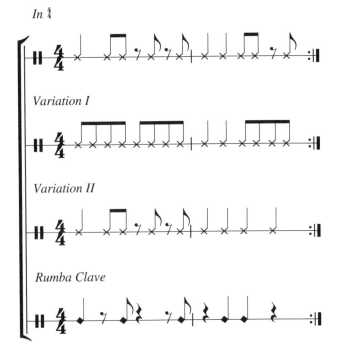

Pilón

Pilón is a dance based on the motions of pounding sugarcane and was made popular by Enrique Bonne in the 1960s. This rhythm is from the eastern part of Cuba.

In ²⁄₄

Bongós/Congas

Timbales

2-3 Clave

In ⁴⁄₄

Bongós/Congas

Timbales

2-3 Clave

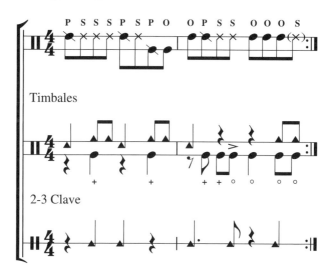

Plena

Plena is a Puerto Rican rhythm that
incorporates African and Spanish elements.
Traditional plena is played with a percussion
ensemble, *cuatro* (four-stringed folk guitar),
and accordion.

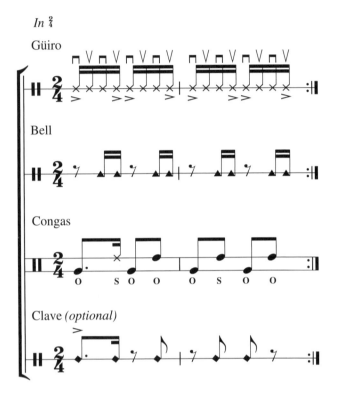

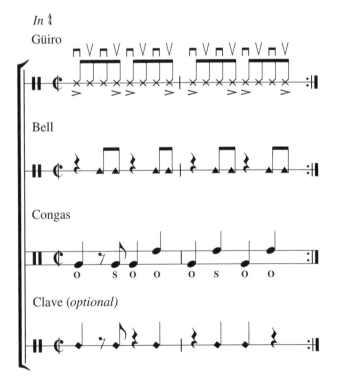

Rumba

Rumba is an Afro-Cuban style that consists of folk percussion rhythms that accompany singers and dancers. The most popular rumba rhythms are: *guaguancó, yambú* and *columbia*.

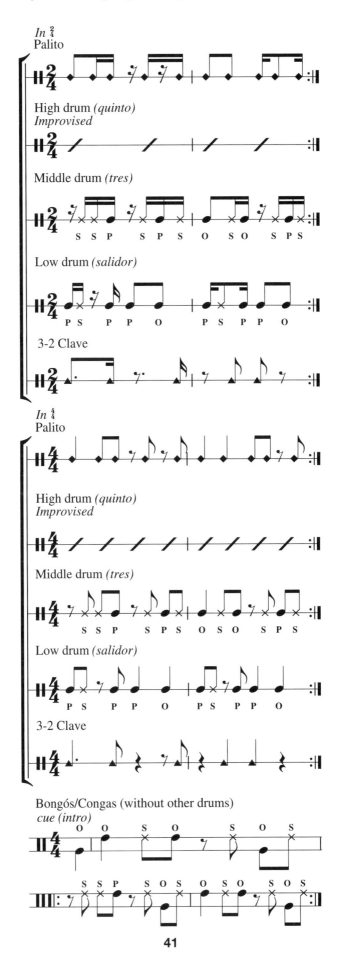

Samba

Samba is the most popular Afro-Brazilian rhythm. There are different variations depending on the region, but all of them have their origin in Congolese and Angolan rhythms. The main characteristics of this style are: an accented beat 2; a percussion ensemble of drums, tambourine and cowbells; and $\frac{2}{4}$ meter. Here are some of the most popular sambas from different parts of Brazil:

Samba

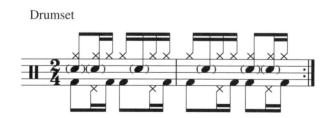

Samba

Samba-Choro

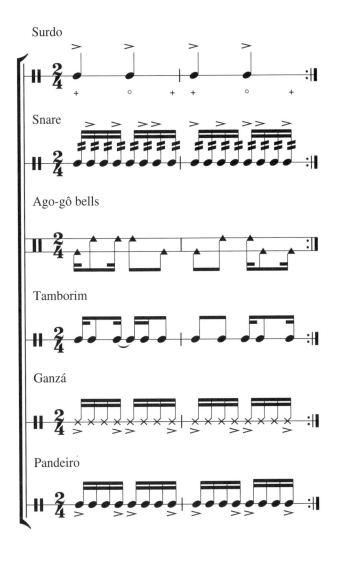

Drumset

Samba

Samba de partido alto

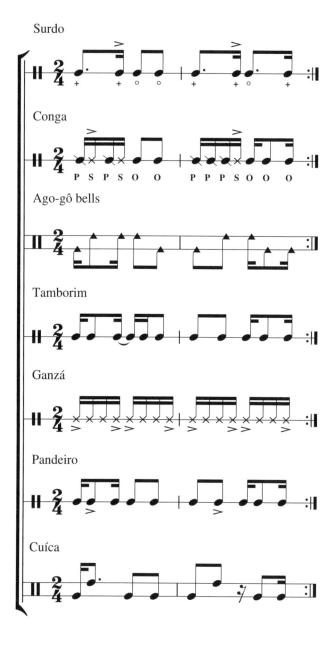

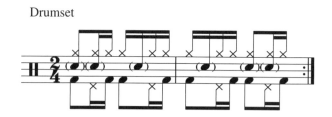

Ska

Ska is a Jamaican rhythm that emerged around the 1950s. It is a mix of rock and roll, jazz, and rhythm and blues, with a feel that is very similar to reggae, since both rhythms emphasize beat 3 of each measure. Another characteristic is the "four on the floor" pulse in the bass drum.

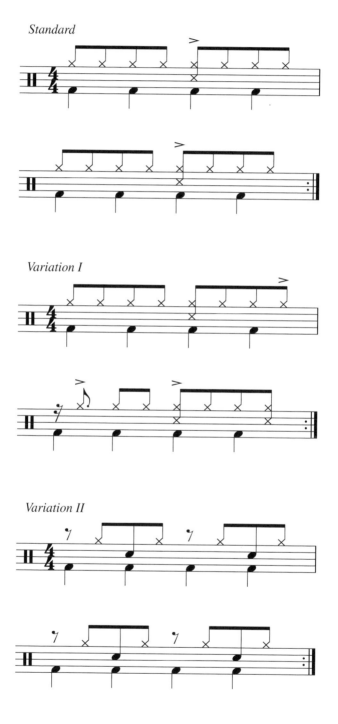

Soca

Soca is a rhythm from the island of Trinidad that became popular in the 1970s. It is basically a faster and modern version of calypso.

Standard

Variation I

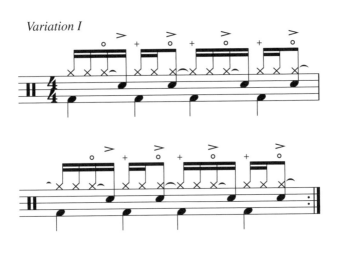

Variation II

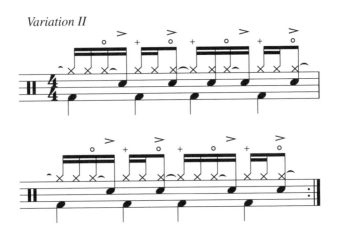

Son

Son is the most influential Cuban style. Started
in the second half of the nineteenth century in
the eastern province of Oriente, son combines
Spanish elements of the *canción* style with
African rhythm and percussion. Early forms
were interpreted by the *campesinos* (peasants)
and developed by the changüí groups.

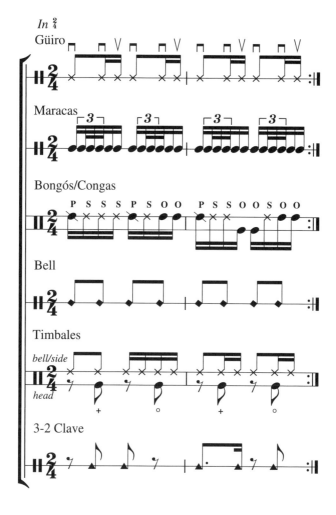

Son

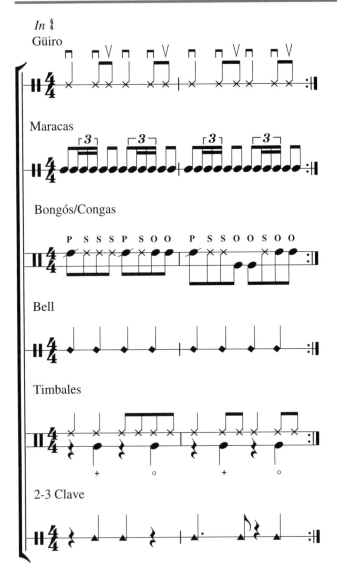

In $\frac{4}{4}$

Güiro

Maracas

Bongós/Congas

Bell

Timbales

2-3 Clave

Songo

Songo is an Afro-Cuban rhythm created by Jose Luis "Changuito" Quintana of Cuba's premiere son group: Los Van Van. This is one of the first Afro-Cuban rhythms created specifically for the drumset.

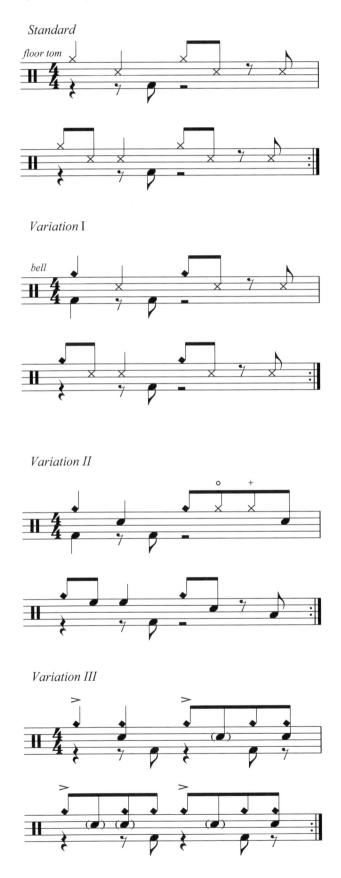

Sucu-Sucu

Sucu-sucu is a variation of Cuban son. Originally from the Isla de Juventud, sucu-sucu was a party rhythm that eventually became a style of its own. The traditional instrumentation of sucu-sucu is tres, bass (or marímbula), machetes, güiro, maracas, cowbell, bongós and conga.

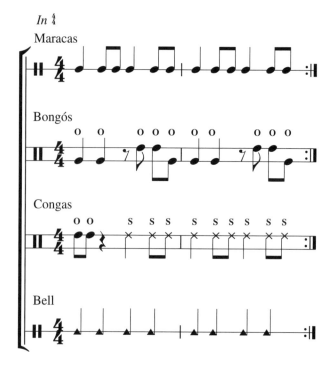

Tango

Tango is the traditional music and dance of Argentina. Written below for drumset, this nineteenth-century rhythm was originally played with castanets. Tango music is traditionally played by an *orquesta típica,* an ensemble comprised of violin, piano, guitar, flute, and *bandoneón* (a hexagonal chromatic accordion).

Vallenato

Vallenato is a Colombian folk rhythm very similar to cumbia. Vallenato's main instruments include the *caja* (percussion box), a *guacharaca* (a kind of güiro), and accordion. The emphasis of this rhythm falls on the strong beats.

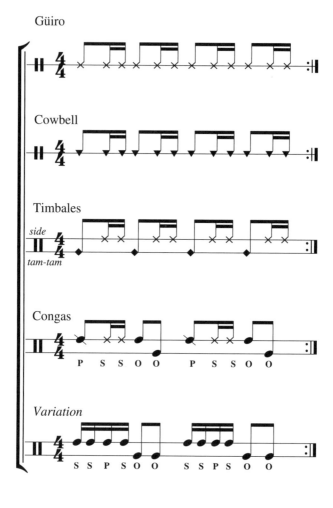

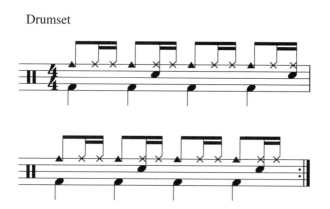

Zydeco

Zydeco is a Afro-Caribbean rhythm played with a button accordion (or the less-traditional keyboard accordion), and a *frottoir* (a rubboard percussion instrument worn on the chest).

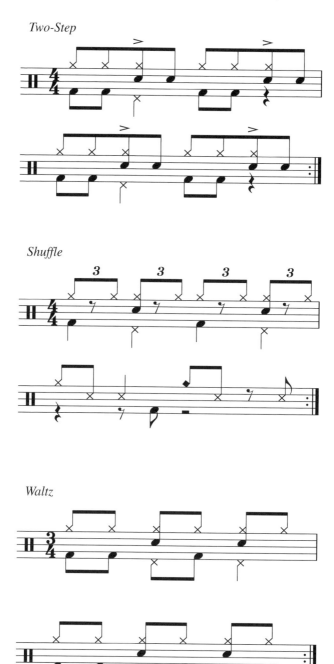

Two-Step

Shuffle

Waltz

Tuning and Maintaining Percussion Instruments

Tuning is the process of producing or preparing to produce a certain pitch in relation to another pitch. Since most percussion instruments are non-pitched, tuning refers to the relative highness or lowness of each instrument and serves to accentuate or diminish certain overtones according to taste.

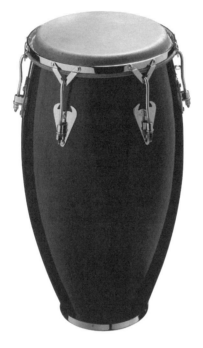

Congas

There are no standard pitches for these instruments. The tuning process for these drums is usually set by style, genre, and tradition. *Congeros* (conga players) train their ears over time to know what kind of sound they want out of their instruments.

The most common tunings for these instruments are done with approximate pitch intervals of thirds, fourths (most popular), and fifths.

Step 1: Cleaning and Preparation

Remove the old skin from the conga and clean the edge of the shell thoroughly (household window cleaner works great). If you notice any defects in the shell, such as cracks, splinters, unevenness, etc., take the drum to your local drum technician for repair. Avoid trying to repair the drum yourself; if you do not know how to fix it properly, you could completely ruin the drum. The process is very detailed since the drum needs to be calibrated, sealed, and braced.

Tuning and Maintaining Percussion Instruments

Step 2: New Skins (Drum Heads)

Make sure that the skin is dry, flat, relatively soft (depending on the make), and that it is not damaged. The new skin should encircle both the wooden shell and the metal hoop. Place the skin on top of the shell, then place the hoop on top of the skin.

Tighten each tension rod/claw manually until you feel the tension is even in all of the rods. The lugs have to be adjusted one at a time, always tuning the next lug located opposite of the first (180° away). By tuning in this manner, we achieve uniform tension on all sides of the drum head. This tuning process is known as *opposite-lug sequence (see below)*.

Step 3: Fine Tuning

Play the head with all the different types of techniques (palm, hand, slaps, open- and closed-tone strokes, finger strokes, etc.) and fine-tune using the opposite-lug tuning sequence. Strive for a warm, deep, and clear conga sound.

Conga Tuning Tips

When tuning your congas, make sure you obtain a pitch that has plenty of sustain when hitting it with an open stroke. This will help reduce undesired overtones.

If you play with two or more congas, try tuning them in thirds, fourths, or fifths for melodic and harmonic consistency.

Tune the congas slowly so that you can notice the differences in tone. Again, try all kinds of strokes with each tuning increment.

When finished playing, tune your congas down a considerable amount. This will extend the life of your heads and will help to fine-tune your ears. This will also allow you to experiment with different tunings each time you play.

Change your heads when the sound of your drums becomes dull, before a recording session, or every few months if you are playing frequently.

Tuning and Maintaining
Percussion Instruments

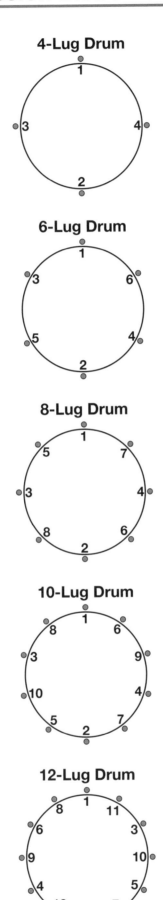

4-Lug Drum

6-Lug Drum

8-Lug Drum

10-Lug Drum

12-Lug Drum

Tuning and Maintaining Percussion Instruments

Bongós

Just like congas, there are not any standard pitches for this instrument. *Bongoceros* (bongo players) tune by ear according to style, genre, and tradition.

Bongos are commonly tuned to the approximate pitch intervals of fourths, fifths (most popular), and octaves.

Step 1: Choosing the Right Head

There are several varieties of skins (heads) to choose from:

Hand Tuck Natural (flat) Skins. These skins need to be hand-tucked. In order to use and tune these types of skins, you need to wet the skin to soften it, and then mount it into the bongos. When purchasing these types of heads, check that both the surface and the thickness of the skins are even.

Mountable Natural (rawhide) Skins. These skins are the most popular since they are already sized and fitted, ready to mount and tune.

Mountable Synthetic Skins. These heads are usually made of a variety of flexible plastic materials. Because they can be tuned higher, these skins will make your bongos sound brighter and louder.

Step 2: Tuning the Heads

Refer to **Steps 2** and **3** of the conga tuning section for specific instructions. If you are using natural skins, make sure that the skins are dry before starting the opposite-lug sequence. Some people like to tune in a clockwise direction, but the opposite-lug sequence distributes the tension in a more even manner, thus helping you achieve a more accurate tuning.

The *macho* (smaller) drum head must be tuned very tightly in order to get a sharp and crisp open tone. The *hembra* (larger) drum must be tuned at a lower pitch, such as a fifth or an octave below the *macho*.

Tuning and Maintaining Percussion Instruments

Bongó Tuning Tips

Apply lug oil before reinserting the tuning lugs. This will make the tuning process easier and prevent the lugs from seizing.

Tighten the head as much as needed. Well-tuned bongos produce a nicer tone than loosely tuned ones.

Weather will most certainly affect the tuning of natural skins. The pitch will rise in warm weather and drop in cold weather. Always make sure that your tuning is correct before you start playing or recording.

Detune your drums after playing. This will extend the life of your heads and fine-tune your ear. This will also allow you to experiment with different tunings every time you play.

It is not necessary to detune synthetic heads, but this is still a good procedure to follow since detuning also keeps tension off the drum shell.

Change your heads when the sound of your instrument is not as bright, before recording, or every few months if you are playing often.

Glossary

Abakwa (Abacuá or Abakuá). This rhythm was developed by a secret fraternal society of the African Carabalí people in Cuba. This musical style influenced other popular genres such as the rumba and guaguancó.

Afoxé. 1. Religious music from the Yoruba tribe. 2. A *cabasa* (squash or pumpkin) covered with a net of shells that is used as a shaker.

Ago-gô. A double bell played with a stick or metal beater. The shape of this bell is triangular (conical), connected by a piece of bent metal, and tuned a relative fourth (or sometimes a fifth) apart. Some ago-gôs are made of three or more bells with different tunings.

Apanpichao. Third (or swing) section of the merengue rhythm.

Banda. A traditional Mexican brass ensemble musical form, banda became popular around the 1960s in Sinaloa, Mexico. It achieved its peak popularity in the late 1990s throughout Mexico and in the southwest United States — especially in Texas, California and, to a lesser degree, in Iowa, Kansas, and Illinois.

Batucada. Samba played by percussion instruments only. Batucada is loud and energetic, and usually played by a large street-samba ensemble.

Bembé. 1. Popular Afro-Cuban § rhythm. Bembé(s) is the African word used for religious gatherings that include drumming, singing and dancing in honor of Orisha. 2. Traditional drums made from hollowed palm tree logs with nailed-on skins tuned with heat and used in the bembé ceremonies.

Bolero (Cuban). Afro-Cuban ballad with a moderate-slow tempo in which the lyric content is mostly romantic. Pepe Sánchez has been credited with creating the Cuban bolero in 1885 with a composition called "Tristeza."

Glossary

Bomba. 1. Puerto Rican folk musical form and dance with African influence. 2. Large barrel-shaped drums similar to, but smaller than, the tumbadora, used to play the bomba rhythm.

Cajón. Box made from wood used in Cuban and Spanish music as a percussion instrument.

Canção. Portuguese for "song."

Canción. Spanish for "song."

Candomblé. A religion that came to Brazil from Africa. The name *Batuque* is also used, especially before the nineteenth century when candomblé became more common. Both words are believed to derive from a Bantu-family language.

Cavaquinho. Small Brazilian guitar made of four metal strings.

Caxixi. Conical-shaped shaker built of basketwork material.

Charanga. Cuban orchestra usually comprised of piano, strings, vocals and percussion. The term also describes a style with the above-mentioned orchestration.

Clave. Rhythmic pattern that is the foundation of most traditional Cuban music.

Claves. Percussion instrument made of two wooden sticks that are used to play the *clave* rhythm.

Columbia. Rumba style played in § and sung with a combination of Spanish and African phrases.

Comparsa. A Cuban party or dance that includes music and dancing, or the band that plays during the celebration.

Congas. Medium-to large-sized drums of Congolese origin (*makuta* drums) used for most Latin-American folk music. The most popular sizes are: the *niño* (25 cm), the *quinto* (28 cm), the *conga*, *seguidor* or *tres golpes* (30

Glossary

cm), and the *tumbadora* (term used in Cuba) or *salidor* (33 cm). Congas are now very common in Latin music.

Conjunto. Traditional Mexican musical style originated in rural northern Mexico in the early twentieth century. This music is based largely on *corridos* and polka. Conjunto and norteño are interchangeable terms used to describe the same style.

Corrido. Narrative song and poetry form of the northern Mexican states that became the most popular style during the Mexican revolution in the early part of the twentieth century. The traditional corrido has a political tone.

Cuatro. A Latin-American guitar-like instrument. The most popular *cuatros* are from Puerto Rico and Venezuela. There are three main types of Puerto Rican cuatros: *Cuatro antigüo* of 4 orders and 4 strings, *Southern cuatro* of 4 orders and 8 strings, and *Cuatro moderno* of 5 orders and 10 strings. The cuatro of Venezuela has four single strings.

Cuica. Brazilian single-headed drum with a rod connected to the underside of the drum head. The rod is pulled with a wet cloth, which creates friction and produces the characteristic sound of the instrument.

Four on the floor. Popular drummer's term that refers to playing four quarter notes on the bass drum consequently and throughout any given rhythm (usually in $\frac{4}{4}$ meter).

Ganzá. Brazilian percussion instrument (shaker) of cylindrical shape filled with stones or pieces of metal.

Gua-gua. Bamboo piece that is mounted and used to play palito patterns.

Guaguancó. An Afro-Cuban music and dance that is a subgenre of the rumba. The dance is traditionally performed by a male and female duo. The male depicts the attempted sexual "capture" of the female by a pelvic thrust called the *Vacunáo*.

Glossary

Güiro. Latin percussion instrument made of a calabash gourd with ridges carved in the skin.

Jaleo. Second section of the merengue rhythm.

Maracas. Hand-held, canister-like rattles with handles played in pairs. Originally made from gourds or dried rawhide and filled with materials such as beads, pebbles and seeds.

Pandeiro. Brazilian tambourine with jingles.

Quebradita. Fast-tempo subgenre of norteño music often performed by a large brass ensemble, vocalists, and percussion.

Quinto. See *congas.*

Ranchera. Slow tempo song subgenre of norteño music. Ranchera instrumentation is usually minimal (e.g., solo guitar).

Repinique (or repique). Brazilian double-headed drum carried over the shoulders, which usually cues the other players.

Salidor. See *congas.*

Salsa. Generic term developed in the late sixties–early seventies used to describe the blending of numerous specific Latin styles into dance orchestra arrangements. The common element in the musical structure is the rhythm pattern of the clave. The word *salsa* means "sauce" in Spanish.

Samba de partido alto (or *Samba de cidade,* "city samba"). In this type of samba, a lead singer improvises verses that alternate with the chorus. The most characteristic feature of this samba is the pandeiro rhythm.

Samba de salão. This saloon (*salão*) samba has a lighter feel than that of *partido alto* and is usually performed with a small ensemble.

Samba-choro. This samba dates to the early nineteenth century. Choro is light music, and often has breaks. The A-B musical form is characteristic of this style.

Glossary

Shekere. African percussion instrument made of a gourd covered with a net of beads (or shells).

Surdo. Brazilian double-headed bass drum. Compared to the zambumba, the surdo is taller.

Tambora. Double-headed drum from the Dominican Republic used in the merengue rhythm. The drum is played with a stick that strikes one head and the wooden shell of the drum, while the hand plays the opposite head.

Tamborim. Brazilian small frame drum played with a stick.

Tejano. The term used in Spanish for "Texan." This style is a combination of various forms of traditional and popular Mexican music with rock, cumbia, and blues, and was created by the descendants of Mexican immigrants in Texas (*Tejanos*). Tex-Mex refers to the more traditional styles such as norteño music. Tejano is usually more modern and is heavily influenced by contemporary popular styles.

Timbal(es). Cuban drums mounted on a stand and played with drumsticks. Measuring in sizes from 13 to 15 inches in diameter, they usually come in pairs, either 13 and 14, or 14 and 15 inches. This instrument is very characteristic of danzón music.

Tres. Small guitar-like instrument, originally from Cuba. The tres can have either three sets of two strings or three sets of three strings. This instrument is highly characteristic of the changüí and son (traditional) styles.

Tres golpes. See *congas*.

Yambú. A type of rumba traditionally performed on the cajón. Yambú is danced by a male-female duo in a slow to medium tempo in duple meter.

Zabumba. Flat, double-headed bass drum originally from Brazil.

STICK IT IN YOUR BAG...

The Stick Bag Book series is an essential collection of easy-to-use reference books for all drummers and percussionists. Written in standard drumset and percussion notation, these clear and concise guides contain the most popular and influential rhythms, patterns, and styles from around the world.

THE STICK BAG BOOK OF WORLD RHYTHM & PERCUSSION
AM985765 $5.95

THE STICK BAG BOOK OF LATIN RHYTHM & PERCUSSION
AM981805 $5.95

THE STICK BAG BOOK OF JAZZ, FUNK & FUSION
AM985776 $5.95

THE STICK BAG BOOK OF RHYTHM & PERCUSSION
AM981816 $5.95

...OR IN YOUR DVD PLAYER

THE ULTIMATE DRUMMER'S WORKOUT
By Ted MacKenzie
Improve your stick technique and gain strength and control through the use of brushes.
DV10505 $14.95

STEPPING IT UP: DEVELOPING STYLE & TECHNIQUE TO ADVANCE THE BEGINNING DRUMMER
By Jamie Borden
Take your basic drum skills and elevate them to the next level.
DV10582 $14.95

Available from your local print music dealer
or **www.musicroom.com**

The **Music Sales** *Group*